The Little Monk

The Little Monk

Wisdom from a Little Friend of Big Faith

Madeleine Delbrêl
Illustrated by Hector V. Lee

A Crossroad Book
The Crossroad Publishing Company
New York

Who is the
Little Monk?

This little book is not a spiritual guidebook. Rather, it is a helpful reminder. The little monk uses these pages to clarify particular events, challenges or nerve wracking experiences of his day. He reflects on his behavior, examines his shortcomings, and jots down a couple of words that he wants to keep in mind.

He himself might have called this "a few memos-to-myself."

The little monk is the sort of person who can make a big deal about things, but in the end doesn't take himself too seriously. This explains the lighthearted way in which the little monk reconsiders events he may have overreacted to at the time.

Now it seems fair to ask: "Who is the little monk?"

To say "the little monk is a flesh-and-blood person" would be dishonest. But to say he never existed isn't true either. While there was never *the* little monk, his character was molded from living people, and his joys and troubles are experienced by many everywhere, everyday.

Indeed, just as there are villages in every corner of the globe, there is a Christian village. But those who dwell in *this* Christian village can't be found in a single region of the world, or in a single branch of the Church. This village consists of rich and poor people alike—some with average intelligence and some with average narrow-mindedness; the strong and the weary; the resourceful and the clumsy; the sought-after and the servile.

In this little village, there are grandfathers and youngsters, aging moms and future grooms, new families and broken marriages.

There are fathers and bachelors, parish priests and bishops, celebrities and transients, and perhaps a sprinkling of congressmen, bankers and tax collectors, abbesses and novice monks, nuns and clergymen. A few people from this village have even become popes or saints.

The little monk is not one person; he is a whole host of people.

He represents those members of the Christian village who are not striving to be elevated as saints—but simply want to live as holy people.

May God take pleasure in us who follow
in the footsteps of the little monk!

I

The Little Monk

The Book of the Beginner

Discernment in action

Do everything as if it were your only passport to heaven.

(When the little monk was in a hurry.)

Worldly noise

When the phone rings, expect a call from God.

(The little monk, upon receiving a phone call at 11:30 P.M.)

Attitude

Better to stand up to things than just to stand them.

(When the little monk couldn't stand either his brothers or himself.)

Holy sloth

Go ahead and relax—just be sure to relax in God.

(When the little monk was feeling lazy.)

Having fun

When you can't dance, let your soul tango.

(The little monk after a day's struggle with accounting.)

Mortification

Unless you're in charge of the kitchen, don't ask for extra salt or sugar, or to reheat your food.

(When the little monk really didn't like the soup.)

Heroism

Hop out of bed the very moment your alarm clock rings.

(The little monk one morning at 6:30 A.M.)

Prefer doing great things with others and serving all to doing greater things alone and serving just yourself.

(The little monk one day when he yearned for the sublime.)

Joy

Do not measure your joy by the well-being of your body.

(When the little monk had heartburn.)

Crises

Bypass them and they'll pass you by.

(The little monk, when feeling blue.)

Confession

Remember that remedies are made for illnesses, not illnesses for remedies!

(When the little monk began using confession as a feel-good medicine.)

Prayer

Remember—the purpose of prayer is to make you a good person, not to keep you from becoming good.

(When the little monk's prayer was interrupted with a request for help.)

Duty

Don't try to recognize duty by the pleasure it brings—
you may never recognize it at all.

(When the little monk had some mending to do.)

Human frailty

Don't lash out—you'll hurt yourself less.

(When the little monk elbowed a brother.)

Language

Don't call "touchiness" in your neighbor what you call "sensitivity" in yourself.

(When someone had hurt the little monk's feelings.)

The Book of the Advanced

Holy poverty

Don't cling to anything—including poverty.

(When the little monk didn't think that his room should be heated.)

Better to take what you are offered, than to choose what you will give up.

(When they poured the little monk a glass of sweet Muscat wine.)

Obedience

Don't wait until you agree with your superior before
obeying him.

(When the little monk believed that he was right.)

Obedience has a little to do with the flesh and a lot to do
with the heart.

*(When the little monk moaned about doing what he was
told to do.)*

Humility

Better not to look at yourself, than to weep over your shortcomings.

(When the little monk wished to examine his conscience.)

Better to accept a mediocre compliment from others than a deliberate criticism from yourself.

(When the little monk was praised for qualities he found of no particular value.)

Remember that you are just like everybody else.

(When the little monk started a diary to record his unique adventures.)

Have no set concept of yourself.

(When the little monk was searching for his identity.)

Silence

Rather than trying to keep quiet, listen.

(When the little monk had some interesting things to say.)

Hold your tongue when you can, so that you can speak when you must.

(When the little monk had some silly little stories to tell.)

True silence never offends love.

(When the little monk responded in monosyllables to a person who bored him.)

Short prayer

My God, let me be willing to hear from others what I can never stop telling myself .

The Book of the Perfect

The love of God

To love God means to be who God wants and do what God wants.

(When the little monk was in a dreamy mood.)

If you cannot love God's holiness by being good, try to love his mercy—even when being bad.

(When the little monk had done foolish things.)

In the company of God within me I serve God within others.

(When the little monk wanted to turn from his brothers.)

There is nothing to fear when you make a habit of wanting to save the whole world at all times.

(When the little monk had to go to the dentist.)

While doing many things you get nothing done, but much gets done by doing the same thing all day long.

(When the little monk felt a desire to go to the Sahara.)

When you misbehave, take pleasure in seeing well-mannered people.

(When his neighbor's calmness exasperated the little monk.)

Don't be a hero—be a zero.

(When the little monk found himself to be mediocre.)

Better to spend your time responding to God than to ask God questions.

(When the little monk was wondering what God thought of him.)

Stop obsessing about doing all of God's will, rather, wish that all would be doing God's will.

(When the little monk was feeling overzealous.)

Not a great saint, and not a great sinner—simply be one more member of the great community called church.

(The little monk when reflecting on his flaws.)

Imagine that you are hollow—you only know how to receive

(When the little monk was seeking a calling.)

The Apprentice Years of the Little Monk

The day you enter the monastery marks not an arrival but a departure.

> *(After the celebrations honoring his entry into the monastery when the little monk felt a desire to sit down and rest.)*

If you don't have a particular burden to carry, you might be meant to help others carry theirs.

> *(When the little monk was quite content with having few responsibilities.)*

Better to pray for others than to judge them.

(When the little monk's nerves were being tested.)

Be yourself whatever you want others to be—only more so.

(When the little monk wanted his brothers to be saints.)

You are always on call.

(When the little monk didn't want to be inconvenienced.)

To serve others is to reign with God.

(When the little monk yearned for heaven.)

When with your brothers behave as if they had only you to lean on, but you had only God.

> *(When the little monk thought that his turn to serve came up too often.)*

No matter where you are, remember that you are all love.

> *(When the little monk mistook mediocrity for humility.)*

Pray to God as if you were the only one doing so.

> *(When all went wrong in the family.)*

When you feel as though you were just the pat of butter used to grease the pan, remember that without the fat the food will burn.

(When the little monk felt humiliated.)

Open your eyes to the suffering around you, yet close them to your own.

(On a day of crisis.)

The Little Monk as Leader

"O crux ave!"
(The little monk when becoming a leader.)

Justice

Beware of how you judge those who do not appreciate you.

(When he felt treated like a nobody.)

When the ones you lead do not confide in you, take a very long time before concluding that they have poor judgement.

(When the little monk had to deal with a few numskulls in his monastery.)

Seek out the company of those who don't like you, and you'll get an opportunity to be fair.

(When the little monk found himself charging others rather than being in charge.)

Don't judge the faults of your children by the indignation
they cause you, but by the pain they cause God.

(When one of his monks behaved badly.)

Put yourself in the shoes of others; don't force them to
wear yours.

*(When the little monk dictated rules of spiritual
discipline.)*

Leaving will make your children envious but only if your heart does not stay with them.

(When, upon returning late to the monastery, the little monk found his sons sulking.)

If you have a bad memory, don't forget to use a pen and paper.

(When the little monk reminded someone of an order that he had neglected to give.)

Humility

To shine is not the same thing as to enlighten.

(On a day of great eloquence.)

Know that it is very fortunate for a monastery to have an incompetent leader when, upon confessing his incompetence, he leaves it up to God.

(One disastrous day.)

Make sure that people don't name the monastery after you, instead of a saint.

(When the little monk became a celebrity in the neighborhood.)

The center of the monastery is God's place: don't put yourself in the wrong chair.

(When the little monk had been pontificating.)

Accept that at times you will get in the way of your brothers—thus becoming a cross to bear, and thus becoming grace.

(When the little monk could not please everybody.)

If the righteous sin seven times a day, don't be surprised —even though you are a leader—that you sin seven times and a half.

(On a discouraging day.)

When certain people question your character, don't respond by doubting theirs.

(When some awfully correct folks told the little monk why he was wrong.)

Peace

Your children didn't come to the monastery to engage in your personal drama.

(When the little monk was down.)

Your attitude reflects the beat of your heart. Love, and your face will be like a fresh, wrinkle-free apron.

(When they said that the little monk had an attitude.)

You haven't reached perfection yet, so don't push others towards it.

(When the little monk wished to speed things up.)

Let God take over. Then *you* take action—if there's still anything to act upon.

(*When the little monk had come up with new ideas for his monks.*)

May each time you return to the monastery seem like an advent of peace.

(*When the little monk returned to find things at odds.*)

Authority

If your child acts like a fool, don't pretend to be an angel
—you might make a fool of yourself.

(When the little monk was trying to demonstrate his virtue.)

Don't confuse God's will with your own.

(When the little monk had ideas about starting a reform.)

Don't forget that weakness is the fear of getting hurt.

(When the little monk decided not to go through with a necessary reproach.)

While authority has its limits, love does not.

(The little monk, meditating on his duties.)

Just because you are in a good mood, do not treat your children as if they were, too.

(When the little monk felt unusually affable toward those in trying situations.)

Don't forget to obey, even while in command.

(When the little monk let out his fantasies about being the boss.)

Submit to discipline, even when no one is watching you.

(One day when the little monk was by himself, and the prayer bell interrupted him in the midst of an interesting distraction.)

Say the things that need to be said, not the things that you'd like to say.

(When his head was brimming with ideas.)

Beware of being too fond of teaching: a father is not a tutor.

(On a day of sermonizing.)

Your silence may serve your others better than the sound of your words.

(When the little monk had a few too many funny stories to tell).

A monastery is not a circus.

(When the little monk felt called to be a clown.)

Gentleness

A leader's anger does not advance justice.

(A Bible citation that the little monk wanted to put into practice.)

Do not make your nerves the barometer of your house.

(On a stressful day.)

Do not expect others to guess how you feel.

(When they spoke to him with candor.)

The Cross

When you weep for others, are you certain you're not weeping for yourself?

(On a day of anxiety.)

You are here to console, not so much to be consoled.

(When the little monk was drowning in a sea of melancholy.)

When one of your children is troubled, may they look for you. When you are troubled, go and look for God.

(When the little monk would have preferred a dialogue to a monologue.)

Beware of wasting time feeling sorry for yourself.

(When the little monk considered himself the unhappiest of all people.)

Prayer

Have more wishes for your children so that God may have more gifts for them.

(When the little monk was weary of everything and everybody.)

Don't neglect your children in order to curry favor with their Father.

(When the little monk wanted his spirituality to be just between him and God.)

Setting an example

A leader is not a billboard, but he is a cornerstone.

(When the little monk wanted to set a good example.)

Your sins are likely to do more harm than your example does good.

(On a day of sentry duty.)

They have the Lord, the Virgin, and all of the Saints to look up to; they don't need you!

(When the little monk was seeking to make himself more popular.)

Parenting

Don't do spiritual direction, but direct your spirit toward your children.

(On a day of monastic activism.)

Don't spend time counting your vices when you could spend it fostering the virtues of others.

(On a day full of fretting.)

Be hard on your children only if it brings you no joy.

(One day while the little monk was having his mouth washed out with soap.)

Remain a father to those who don't treat you like one.

(When the little monk's efforts were met with failure.)

Finesse

Never say anything to any of your children that may diminish their fondness for a sibling.

(When the little monk had a desire to vent his feelings.)

Don't scratch an abscess and spread the infection.

(On a day of vehemence.)

Don't give orders—ask for services.

(When the little monk felt too lazy to say "Brother So-and-So, would you please be kind enough to . . . ")

II

The Little Monk on Everyday Adventure

The Little Fighter Monk

Community life

These lines are intended not just for monasteries, but also for:

- families
- schools
- workplaces
- governments
- churches
- political parties

. . . In short, for any kind of community.

War and peace

Learn the art of making war on yourself, and the art of making peace with others.

(When a holy fight broke out.)

True zeal does not carry bombs.

(When the little monk was defending his movement.)

If your voice sounds like a bugle, your brother will loathe music.

(During a feisty conversation.)

You may be a fighter, but that does not make your monastery a battlefield.

> *(When the little monk wanted to get everything going at once.)*

Do not think of your adversaries as undefeatable armor.

> *(After a needed rejoinder.)*

Triumphant conduct does not suit holy warriors.

> *(When the little monk was showing off.)*

Strategy is one thing—God's ways are another.

> *(On an evening marred by failure.)*

An activist doesn't need to enlist in the military.

(On a day of particular vigor.)

When you scream, you will deafen your neighbor's ears.

(When no one was listening to the little monk.)

Remember that working on personal growth
is not quite the same as having to do hard
physical labor everyday.

*(On a day of inner struggle and
stormy weather.)*

Our weaknesses

We'd be patient sooner, if we chose patience.

*(When a slap in the face seemed to have no effect
on him.)*

Fragile hearts are good for display; they're hopeless in the
battle for love.

(When someone broke his heart.)

Silence

The first step on the mystic ladder of silence is to avoid listening to yourself.

(The little monk after giving a brilliant speech.)

And the second to last step on this same ladder is listening to others.

(No comment here.)

Silence was made so that we can listen to God. When God speaks through his creatures, don't cut him off.

(At the bedside of a brother who at old age had returned to talking like a little child.)

Greatness

The little monk was a child of his time—that is to say, of our own. He was enthusiastic about contemporary efforts to promote human greatness. And for his love of humanity and for its honor and for its glory he sought to become great himself.

In this respect, counsel from the gospel had confused him since the beginning of his career. In some obscure way, he felt as if he was asked to compromise his rich personality.

It was then that he wrote these notes:

If you want to be humble, don't belittle the greatness of others.

(When the little monk was bothered by the admiration offered to others.)

When you finally discover that you are just one of the little people, don't conclude that this makes you special.

(After a few remarkable insights into his insignificance.)

To call oneself "humble" rarely means that one *is* humble; the truly humble know that they are but novices in matters of humility.

(When the little monk had been self-effacing all around.)

If you can't admire your righteousness, don't admire your regret.

(When the little monk shut himself away to attend to his remorse.)

The stature of celebrities doesn't change at all who you are; it is because God is great that you are little.

(When the little monk's heart was pounding with affirmation.)

Don't reach the state of modesty as if you had just won the Tour de France.

(When the little monk was overwhelmed by his own humbleness.)

Be modest, but do not think you're worth per ounce what your brother is worth per pound.

(See above.)

Hygiene

It matters to know the difference between the stupor of our spirit and the condition of our body.

(On a sad day.)

If you lose your face, persevere; if you lose your head, halt.

(On a day jam-packed with contradictions.)

If your heart goes to your head, far too much has been going on.

(When the little monk felt overwhelmed.)

More than six billion people bear the burden of life; it helps to know that you're no exception.

(When the little monk was fighting off sleep.)

Giving advice—or, walking in another's shoes.

"Givers of advice don't pay the price."

(A proverb the little monk cherishes, and one he keeps in mind whenever counseling people.)

It shows no respect of humanity to let your brother behave like a fool.

(When the little monk held back discretely.)

Keep in mind that just living with you may serve as enough penance to get into heaven.

(On a day of bitter words.)

Even when an adult, you're still a child of God.

(The little monk, meditating on the importance of his responsibilities.)

When you say to your brother "I'll take charge of your bundle," he'll be happy. But when you say "I'll take charge of you," he will not.

(When the little monk felt great educational zeal.)

When you treat your brother like a child, it is because you have grown too old.

(The little monk, crooked from bending down to attend to others.)

O God of great counsel!
Make me comprehend that I am no God,
and that my advice
is modest advice indeed!
Amen.

The Little Monk as Missionary

Don't forget that you chose what you want others
to accept.

> *(When the little monk thought he was just like the
> indigenous that surrounded him.)*

If you are just like others, you can't bring them
anything new.

> *(When, in order to bring God to the people, the little
> monk equated himself to them in everything.)*

And if you gave the moon and the stars to your friends, it would not move them any closer to heaven.

(When the little monk liked to give others gifts that he really would have wanted to receive himself.)

Think that you are right, but don't quite believe it.

(When the little monk defended something he was right about.)

When your behavior upsets others, change it. However, should you find it necessary to change your clothes, don't barter Christ.

(When the little monk was exploring ways to share his faith.)

A tear may be worth as much as a drop of blood—but not every tear is.

(When the little monk felt grossly ignored.)

If martyrdom is what you are looking for, you might as well do your work while waiting.

(When the little monk had to prepare his taxes.)

When you want to preach, remember: a crowd might be hard of hearing; yet, a person has two ears.

(At a gathering.)

The Holy Spirit is always on the move—don't block the pulley.

(When the little monk wished he didn't have to write to his bishop.)

When you want others to love the ones you love; love the ones who do not love them.

(When the little monk engaged in peacemaking.)

God may want separation, but He never wants division.

(When certain relations were dampening the little monk's apostolic zeal.)

Carry the community and it will carry you.

(When the little monk was not in the mood for being a saint.)

Jesus did not condemn the rich. He condemned those who assume that their wealth releases them from their responsibilities to the community.

(When the little monk turned to the Bible—seeking an excuse for turning his back on a banker.)

Christ never cursed anyone for being a banker, but he condemned those who judge others.

(See above.)

When your pocketbook is too small to hold the whole Gospel, take your backpack.

(When the little monk, out of love for the poor, threw out the rich.)

It is easier for others to relieve you of your greatest burden—make sure that you thank God for them daily.

(When the short-lived career of the little monk was unjustly ended by the strike of a pen.)

The Ordeals of an Ordinary Believer

The noonday demon

What you chose to advance your faith will be the very thing that you will hate about the faith.

(The little monk after having lived ten years among his brothers.)

Indeed, experience has shown that these same words are

- *spoken*
- *yelled*
- *whispered*
- *sobbed*

by

- *women to their husbands, after ten years of marriage*
- *husbands to their wives on their tenth wedding anniversary*
- *doctors after ten years of practice*
- *activists after ten years of protest*
- *missionaries after ten years of preaching*
- *any believer at the end of ten years of believing.*

Note that certain deviations were observed regarding the time frame. Depending on the case ten years may be seven or thirteen. However, everybody has the impression that it is ten years.

(Madeleine Delbrêl on a miserable day.)

Life with God

Retreats

While on retreat, sleep is a necessary activity; but it is a good idea to pursue other activities, as well.

(As the little monk was preparing for prayer.)

The tender breeze of the Spirit does not necessarily smell like mimosa.

(When the little monk was making plans for a retreat in a sunny place.)

The fragrance of the fields is no more conducive to God than the rattle of a bus.

(Still working on a place for his retreat.)

It was never a preferential option for God to dwell in historical monuments.

(Still making up his mind . . .)

If you are a gifted comedian, beware of glitzy stage décors.

(Still deciding . . .)

Prayer

Distractions become prayers when we keep with God.
However, resisting them can make us more distracted.

(In times of overload.)

You lack nothing that's needed to tell God what He
wants, however, you lack much that is needed to tell God
what you want.

*(When the little monk lacked time, space, silence, and
many more things.)*

Talk to God rather than to yourself; at least it will give you extra prayertime.

(When the little monk was sharing a few thoughts with himself.)

When you believe that God is living with you, wherever you have room to live, you will have room to pray.

(When the monastery was hazardously overcrowded.)

When you go to the ends of the earth, you will find traces of God; if you go to the depths of your soul, you will find God Himself.

(When the little monk dreamt about finding God.)

It takes a lot of effort and a lot of deliberation to find petroleum; why, then, do we hope to find God with little deliberation and little effort?

(The little monk on praying during a storm.)

God has wisdom when you might not. But God has no headaches and yours could actually be brought to his service.

(One day when pain in his body was clouding his mind.)

Prayer does not mean being intelligent—it means
being present.

    (When paying heed to people chatting on the street.)

To find God, it serves to know that He is everywhere, it also serves to know that He is not alone.

(The little monk gladly used this saying when a bunch of things interested him, or when a bunch of people annoyed him.)

When you long for the desert, remember that God prefers people.

(While reciting his rosary in the subway.)

Changing monasteries does not change the monk, and changing locations does not change God.

(The little monk, standing in front of a travel agency.)

For he who seeks God as Moses did, a staircase can resemble the Sinai.

(At every step on every floor.)

My God, if you are everywhere, why then am I somewhere else so frequently?

(Short prayer to be recited now and then.)

Who is Madeleine Delbrêl?

Madeleine Delbrêl was born in 1904 in Mussidan, a small town in the south of France. Her father was of an artistic disposition, and Madeleine inherited his interest in and talent for writing. Throughout her childhood, she lived in several different places, never able to feel at home or make friends anywhere. Her parents were not religious, so that Madeleine was an atheist by the age of fifteen, experiencing life as absurd. At seventeen she wrote a tract titled: "God is dead—long live death!" which expresses her view that death is the only certainty in life.

Consequently, she lived life to the fullest, writing and illustrating poetry, studying philosophy and art at the Sorbonne in Paris, designing her own (shock-provoking) clothes, and being one of the first women of her society to cut her hair short.

However, when her fiancé suddenly decided to join the Dominicans and her father went blind, her life fell apart. At the same time she noticed that life did not seem absurd to her Christian friends, who still enjoyed life as much as she did. Suddenly God's existence did not seem a complete impossibility anymore. She decided to kneel and pray, also remembering Teresa of Avila's recommendation to silently think of God for five minutes each day.

Madeleine called 1924 the year of her conversion. For in praying she found God—or as she felt, he found her. To her he was someone to love just like any other person. At first she considered taking the veil and entering the Carmelite order, but then felt called upon to be in touch with people and help them lead a happier life. She joined the Girl Scouts, then led a group of women in Ivry, a small working-class town, with the goal of simply caring, consoling, aiding, and established good contact with the people. She then took a degree in Social Studies and was employed by the city government of Ivry, where she worked throughout World War II and thereafter.

During this time she came in contact with communism. Although it encouraged brotherhood between people in the working class, she rejected it because it excluded everybody else from the charity she felt was due to everyone.

Characteristic for her ideal of charity was the "open house" with doors from which no one was ever rejected.

Madeleine died unexpectedly from a brain hemorrhage in 1964.

During her lifetime, Madeleine published various writings. *The Little Monk* is a collection of aphorisms that was already circulating among her friends during her lifetime and intended for publication, but her sudden death prevented her from accomplishing this.

Crossroad is honored to introduce *The Little Monk* in English for the first time.

Memos to Myself

Memos to Myself

Memos to Myself

Memos to Myself

Contents

Who Is the Little Monk?   5

The Little Monk   9

     The Book of the Beginner   11

     The Book of the Advanced   25

     The Book of the Perfect   31

     The Apprentice Years of the Little Monk   35

     The Little Monk as Leader   39

The Little Monk on Everyday Adventure   65

     The Little Fighter Monk   67

     The Little Monk as Missionary   83

     The Ordeals of an Ordinary Believer   91

     Life with God   93

Who is Madeleine Delbrel?   107

Memos to Myself   111

The Crossroad Publishing Company
16 Penn Plaza, 481 Eighth Avenue
New York, NY 10001

Copyright © 2005 by The Crossroad Publishing Company
Text excerpted from original work *Alcide: Guide simple pour simple chretiens*
by Madeleine Delbrêl, Copyright © 1997 Editions du Seuil.

Translation by Carol C. Macomber of The French Connection.

Illustrations by Hector V. Lee.

Printed in Singapore.

The text of this book is typeset in Granjon.
The display face is in Papyrus.

Cataloging-in-Publication Data is available from the Library of Congress
ISBN 0-8245-2310-5

2 3 4 5 6 7 8 9 10   10 09 08 07

Of Related Interst

Theophane the Monk
Tales from a Magic Monastery
Illustrated by John O'Brien

"In the tradition of the masters Father Theophoane seeks to put us in touch with some of the deepest mysteries of life through the medium of story. Like the parables of Jesus, these tales repeatedly unfold new levels of meaning if we are willing to sit with them. The use of the story is the rediscovery of our times and the Monk Theophane (an experienced retreat director and a true spiritual father) is a master of the art."—M. Basil Pennington, O.C.S.O.

ISBN 0-8245-0085-7, $13.95, paperback

Paula D'Arcy
A New Set of Eyes
Encountering the Hidden God

Since the sudden death of her husband and young daughter to a drunk-driving accident in 1977, Paula D'Arcy has been on a personal quest to get answers from God. At the time, she was a young wife and mother in her twenties and three months pregnant. She thought her life was over. She told the story of her journey from despair over those horrifying losses back to faith in a loving God in her book, *Gift of the Red Bird*.

Now, as a much-sought-after retreat master and spiritual director, D'Arcy is helping women and men discover the hidden God within themselves by sharing insights from her personal journey. *A New Set of Eyes* provides readers with a series of parables, meditations and directives that are designed to awaken the mind to the presence of God, free the soul from it's cherished idols, and infuse the emotions with their birthright of joy.

ISBN 0-8245-1930-2, $16.95, hardcover

Henri Nouwen
Life of the Beloved
Spiritual Living in a Secular World

Over 200,000 copies in-print!

When Nouwen was asked by a secular Jewish friend to explain his faith in simple language, he responded with *Life of the Beloved*, which shows that all people, believers and nonbelievers, are beloved by God unconditionally. Now with reflection guide.

"Nouwen's prose is refreshingly straight-forward and jargon-free. . . . For those unfamiliar with his work, this latest volume is a wonderful place to begin. For other who have benefited from Nouwen's insights, *Life of the Beloved* will be welcomed as yet another significant achievement."—Circuit Rider

ISBN 0-8245-1986-8, $14.95, paperback

Please support your local bookstore,
or call 1-800-707-0670 for Customer Service.

For a free catalog, write us at:

THE CROSSROAD PUBLISHING COMPANY
16 PENN PLAZA, SUITE 1550
NEW YORK, NY 10001

Visit our website at
www.cpcbooks.com
All prices subject to change.